Our Lady's Psalter

The Rosary of the Mystery of Christ

Translated by
Marco T.

Library and Archives Canada Cataloguing in Publication

Dominic of Prussia, 1382 or 4 - 1460 or 1
  Our Lady's Psalter : The Rosary of the Mystery of Christ

Translated by Marco Testa.
Translated from Latin.
Includes some text in Latin.

ISBN 978-0-9880692-0-6

1. Rosary--Early works to 1800.
2. Mary, Blessed Virgin,
Saint--Devotion to--Early works to 1800.
I. Testa, Marco II. Title.
BX2163.D6613 2012   242'.74   C2012-903295-6

For additional copies:
  email **liturgical.latin@live.ca**

Printed and bound in Canada.

Cover art: Crucifixion
Brother Maximilian Schmalzl, CSSR (1850-1930)
Roman Missal, Regensburg: Verlag Friedrich Pustet, 1926
Design by Joseph DeCaria

Our Lady's Psalter

The Rosary of the Mystery of Christ

CONTENTS

INTRODUCTION

The rosary is arguably the most common form of the Church's extra-liturgical prayer. It is certainly the one most frequently recommended by the popes of the last century. It was St. Pius V who in 1569 officially approved the rosary in its present form. In 2002, with his Apostolic Letter, *Rosarium Virginis Mariae*, Blessed John Paul II explained that "the Rosary, though clearly Marian in character, is at heart a Christocentric prayer. In the sobriety of its elements, it has all the depth of the Gospel message in its entirety, of which it can be said to be a compendium. It is an echo of the prayer of Mary, her perennial *Magnificat* for the work of the redemptive Incarnation which began in her virginal womb. With the Rosary, the Christian people sit at the school of Mary and are led to contemplate the beauty on the face of Christ and to experience the depths of His love. Through the Rosary the faithful receive abundant grace, as though from the very hands of the Mother of the Redeemer."[1] In this same Apostolic Letter the Holy Father further enriched the rosary with

---

[1] John Paul II, Apostolic Letter, *Rosarium Virginis Mariae*, 16 October, 2002.

the Luminous Mysteries; and in so doing, he retrieved an older element in the tradition of this beloved form of prayer.

In its earliest forms the rosary developed as a common method of prayer modeled on the monastic prayer of the Psalms out of a desire to participate in some way in the Church's continual prayer in the Divine Office. The faithful were at first encouraged to pray 150 *Paternosters* (the *Our Father*). At the same time, devotees of our Lady used antiphons in her honour in chaplets of varying number or psalters of 150 replacing the *Pater noster* with Gabriel's *Ave*. Marian Psalters which originated in the twelfth century likewise developed from the recitation of the Psalter in private devotions. In time, as the recitation of the *Hail Mary* became more popular, the rosary became increasingly Marian in its focus. The arrangement that you will find in this book has its origin in German Cistercian and Carthusian monasteries of the fourteenth and fifteenth centuries. Sometime between 1409 and 1415, Dominic of Prussia, a Carthusian monk, composed fifty meditations or clauses (*clausulae*) summarizing the principal mysteries of the life of Jesus. These were recited after the Holy Name of Jesus, ending with *'Amen'*. There is some suggestion that he also authored a collection of one hundred and fifty meditations at a later date. His contribution to the development of the rosary emphasised its use as an aid to meditative prayer rooted in Sacred Scripture and the *imitatio Christi*, the imitation of Christ.

The *clausulae* in this collection[2], are known as the *Oldest Rosary Clausulae*. Though their authorship is uncertain, they are nevertheless representative of the rosary as a continuous meditation on the life, death and resurrection of Jesus Christ with a definite Marian perspective and emphasis. They are inspired by Sacred Scripture, Catholic theology and in some instances, apocryphal literature. In similar manner, monastic practices and virtues are woven into the narrative and our Lady is presented as the exemplar of both the active and particularly, the contemplative life. When praying what we may call the clausular rosary, these brief doctrinal statements or *clausulae* are inserted into the *Hail Mary* after the Holy Name of Jesus. A dialogue of prayer ensues which engages either our Lord Jesus Christ or His Holy Mother in a

---

[2] *Die altesten Rosencranz "Clausulae"*, Kölner Codex Ms. W 4° 119.

conversation that invites one to contemplate the Mystery of the redemptive Incarnation. It is a prayerful dialogue, at once both Marian and Christocentric.

This collection contains the oldest rosary *clausulae* in Latin and their English counterparts. The format facilitates prayer in either language. This volume brings together different traditional elements of a prayer that over centuries has evolved and which still today continues to form the faithful in the Gospel. By combining these deeply spiritual and theological formulae with the *Hail Mary*, the more ancient form of the rosary is wedded to its more recent expression, popularized principally by the Dominican Order and fostered by the papal Magisterium.

This little volume, reminiscent of the *Little Office of the Blessed Virgin Mary, Officium Parvum Beatae Mariae Virginis*, is lovingly dedicated to the Mother of the Redeemer, *Regina Sanctissimi Rosarii*, the Queen of the Most Holy Rosary. As the Church celebrates the Year of Faith, may our Lady, *Virgo fidelis*, the Virgin most faithful, help us and teach us by her faith and example "to rediscover the content of the faith that is professed, celebrated, lived and prayed."[3] May we learn from her whom the ages proclaim "blessed because she believed" (*Lk 1:45*) to contemplate the mystery of Christ and worship the Triune God "in spirit and in truth, for such the Father seeks to worship Him" (*Jn. 4:23*).

---

[3] Benedict XVI, *Porta Fidei,* Apostolic Letter for the Indiction for the Year of Faith, 11 October, 2011.

Translator's Note

The Latin of the *clausulae* reflects Mediaeval Latin spelling and conventions. As noted, the text of some of the *clausulae* is inspired by apocryphal literature, principally; the *Protoevangelium of James*, whose mariological contents adapted by James of Voragine (+1298) in *The Golden Legend* (ca AD 1260-1265) exerted significant influence on western art and iconography. This, for example, is true of *clausulae* 9, 11 & 16. I wish to express my gratitude to Fr. Neil Roy, PhD for his insights into the apocryphal origin and significance of a number of the *clausulae*. Those interested in the history of the rosary may consult Anne Winston-Allen's *Stories of the Rose, The Making of the Rosary in the Middle Ages*.

Rev. Marco Testa

How to Pray
The Clausular Rosary

There are three Psalters or groupings of fifty meditations (*clausulae*) in this collection. Unlike the Dominican rosary which assigns particular mysteries to the different days of the week, the clausular rosary consecrates a particular mystery of the life of Jesus to each *Hail Mary*. As one prays this rosary, the *Our Father* and the *Glory be* may be inserted at the beginning and end of each decade as with the Dominican rosary. Since this form of prayer aims to lead towards contemplation of the Mystery of Christ, the quantity of prayers is not what matters. It is for you to determine the number of themes you wish to contemplate. The text of the *Hail Mary* in both Latin and English is here reproduced as an aid to prayer.

Ave Maria

Ave Maria,
gratia plena,
Dominus tecum.
Benedicta tu
in mulieribus, et
benedictus fructus
ventris tui, Jesus,

Qui...

Sancta Maria,
Mater Dei, ora pro
nobis peccatoribus,
nunc, et in hora
mortis nostrae.

Amen.

Hail Mary

Hail Mary,
full of grace,
the Lord is with thee.
Blessed art thou
amongst women and
blessed is the fruit of
thy womb, Jesus,

Who...

Holy Mary,
Mother of God,
pray for us sinners,
now, and at the hour
of our death.

Amen.

Prima
Quinquagena

First
Psalter

Qui secundum divinitatem etiam est Pater tuus, ipse enim te fundavit Altissimus.

Who according to His divinity is also thy Father; for He the Most High created thee.

Qui te cum Patre et Spiritu Sancto praedestinavit ab aeterno, ab initio enim et ante saecula cara es.

Who with the Father and the Holy Spirit from eternity predestined thee; for from the beginning and before the ages thou art beloved.

Qui te sicut seipsum sine originali concipi voluit, sicut tu revelasti multis et sancta Ecclesia iam credendum instituit.

Who willed that thou be conceived without original sin like He Himself; as thou hast revealed to many and Holy Church has now decreed to be believed.

Qui admirabili consilio in abysso summae Trinitatis praeelegit te in

Who by a wondrous counsel in the abyss of the most Holy Trinity chose thee as Mother

matrem ad totius humani generis salutem.

for the salvation of the whole human race.

 **5**

Qui te ut rosam sine spinis per Patrem in divinis sic sublimavit, ut fieres comparens Patri, et sua sancta parens.

Who through the Father so exalted thee among things divine as a rose without thorns; that thou should be joined to the Father and be His Holy Mother.

 **6**

Qui te per Spiritum Sanctum sic perfecit, ut esses vas divinae bonitatis et totius pietatis ad omnia utilis tam hominibus quam angelis.

Who through the Holy Spirit so perfected thee that thou would be the vessel of divine goodness and all piety, helpful to all, both men and angels.

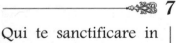 **7**

Qui te sanctificare in utero matris opus non habuit a peccato ut Jeremiam et Johannem, et cum omni sanctitate et gratia te amplius decoravit.

Who did not need to sanctify thee in thy mother's womb as with Jeremiah and John; and who has richly adorned thee with all holiness and grace.

Qui in tua nativitate angelos ineffabiliter gaudere fecit, et toti mundo lucem novam, spem et veniam repromisit.

Who in thy nativity caused the angels ineffably to rejoice and promised anew to the whole world new light, hope and forgiveness.

Qui te domum patris oblivisci, et in templo suo fecit commorari, ut summus rex eo amplius concupisceret speciem tuam et decorem.

Who made thee to forget the house of thy father and made thee to dwell in His Temple; that there the Supreme King might all the more desire thy beauty and comeliness.

Qui eligens esse virginis filius tibi inspiravit, ut virginitatem tu prima sibi devoveres atque virgo perpetua permaneres.

Who, choosing to be the Son of a virgin inspired thee first to vow thy virginity and that thou remain a virgin forever.

| Qui tibi per angelum cibum destinavit, ut Hieronymus scribit. | Who appointed for thee food through an angel, as Jerome writes. |

| Qui te in activa et contemplativa vita perfectam exhibuit, sicut ipse vixit. | Who caused thee to be perfect in both the active and contemplative life, as He Himself did live it. |

| Qui te tam in lege quam prophetis, carminibusque Davidicis plene erudivit. | Who fully instructed thee in the law as well as the prophets and in the songs of David. |

| Qui te pulcherrimam in anima et corpora formavit, ut tamen nullus te impudice concupireret. | Who formed thee most beautifully in soul and in body so that no one might desire thee unchastely. |

Qui te fecit tam inclitam in omni vita, ut omnes per te invitentur ad opera bona.

Who made thee so renowned in all life that through thee, all might be led to good works.

Qui te instruxit, ut rennuens ad sacerdotis vocem nubere, donec per miraculum sanctus Joseph designaretur, et fides tua de virginitate retinenda inde roboraretur.

Who instructed thee, as thou did hesitate to wed at the bidding of the priest, until St. Joseph was designated through a miracle; so that thy vow concerning the keeping of thy maidenhood thenceforth might be strengthened.

Qui tibi suam ostendit voluntatem, ut per sanctam obedientiam permitteres te desponsari.

Who showed thee His will, that through holy obedience He should permit thee to be betrothed.

Qui te honeste sociatam virginibus a sacerdote disposuit reverti ad parentes.

Who arranged that thou who were honourably associated with virgins should be allowed by the priest to return to thy parents.

Qui te fecit etiam ibi amare cellam quietem et solitudinem et sacram lectionem.

Who made thee there to love the quiet of thy cell and solitude and holy reading.

Qui te licet anxiam, tamen de servanda integritate fidelissimam, tunc fecit orare clauso ostio.

Who allowed thee to pray behind closed doors for thou were anxious and most faithful about preserving thy integrity.

Qui ad te desponsatam angelum misit, qui te reverendissime salutavit.

Who sent the angel to thee now betrothed and who greeted thee most reverently.

Qui te ideo ante salutationem desponsatam prius esse voluit, ut diabolus falleretur.

Who wanted thee to be betrothed before the salutation so that the devil might be deceived.

Qui tibi pactum custodivit, ut virgo permanens, et tamen statum matrimonii haberes.

Who guarded the agreement with thee that thou might remain a virgin and that thou should nevertheless have the state of marriage.

Qui iussit angelo, ut te vocaret "gratia plena" novo nomine, quia, sicut Jeremias dixit, novum fecit Dominus super terram: Femina circumdabit virum in utero et non ab extrinseco.

Who commanded the angel to address thee by a new name, "full of grace"; for as Jeremiah said, the Lord has done a new thing on the earth: a Woman will surround a man in the womb and not from without.

25

Qui iussit dicere angelum "Ave gratia plena", quia coelis gloriam, terris Deum pacemque dedisti.	Who commanded the angel to say, "Hail, full of grace", for thou hast given glory to the heavens; God and peace to the earth.

26

Qui ad te angelum ideo misit, quia angelis semper est cognata virginitas.	Who on that account sent the angel to thee, for virginity is always related to angels.

27

Qui te totaliter implevit gratia sua, quam ceteris per partes tribuit.	Who completely filled thee with His grace, which to others He granted in part.

28

Qui iam erat tecum, antequam angelus venit, quia praecessit nuntium suum Deus.	Who was already with thee, before the angel came; for God goes before His messenger.

Qui te sic benedixit, ut omnem maledictionem Evae a mulieribus per te excluderet.

Who so blessed thee that through thee He might take away from women every curse of Eve.

Qui per te a nobis abstulit omne ve et omnia, tam quae in coelis quam quae in terris sunt, benedixit.

Who through thee removed from us all woe and blessed all things both in heaven and on earth.

Qui te pulchram fecit inter filias Jerusalem concupiscens tuam speciem et decorem.

Who made thee so beautiful among the daughters of Jerusalem desiring thy beauty and comeliness.

Qui te replevit caritate et dilectione et omni virtute speciositatis atque splendoris.

Who filled thee with charity and love and every virtue of beauty and splendour.

33

Qui te laetificavit mirum in modum per archangeli novae et inauditae salutationis gaudium.	Who gave thee joy in a wonderful manner through the joy of the archangel's new and unheard of greeting.

34

Qui tibi dederat virginalem verecundiam simul et fortitudinem, quod turbata es et non conturbata in salutatione.	Who had given thee at once virginal modesty and strength because thou were troubled but not disturbed at the angel's greeting.

35

Qui te sic contemplativam effecit, ut solus angelus te solam reperiret legentem et orantem.	Who made thee so contemplative that the angel alone should find thee alone reading and praying.

Qui te virginibus dedit exemplum, ut sicut tu sic et ipsae ad omnis viri affatum timerent.

Who gave thee as an example to virgins that like thee they also might fear every address of man.

Qui tibi talem dederat intellectum et pudorem virgineum, ut tacite cogitares, qualis esset haec salutatio.

Who gave thee such intelligence and virginal purity that inwardly thou should think of the meaning of this greeting.

Qui tibi soli hanc novam salutationem reservaverat, ut gratiae replereris auctore.

Who had reserved this greeting for thee alone, that thou should be filled by the Author of grace.

Qui te per angelum statim consolabatur, ne timeres, quia gratiam Domini perditam reinvenisses.

Who through the angel at once consoled thee lest thou be afraid; so that thou should find again the grace of the Lord which had been lost.

Qui te tua ex humilitate, pudicitia, castitate et conscientiae puritate fecit hanc gratiam invenire.

Who because of thy humility, modesty, chastity and purity of conscience enabled thee to find this grace.

Qui hanc gratiam te fecit invenire, scilicet Dei et hominum pacem, mortis destructionem et vitae reparationem.

Who made thee to find this grace, namely, peace between God and men, the destruction of death and the restoring of life.

Qui promisit te concepturam statim in utero, nihil ab extra recipiendo et ideo sine omni libidine.

Who promised that thou would conceive at once in thy womb; receiving nothing from without and on that account, without any passion.

Qui etiam praenuntiavit tibi nomen Filii, ut eum vocares Jesum, quod est mel in ore, melos in aure, jubilus in corde.

Who even made known to thee the name of thy Son; that thou should call Him Jesus – a name which is honey to the mouth, music to the ear and joy in the heart.

Quem angelus dixit magnum futurum, et in gratiae singularitate, in regali dignitate et vera deitate.

Whom the angel said would be great both in singularity of grace, in royal dignity and true divinity.

Quem angelus dixit habiturum sedem David, id est regnum sanctae Ecclesiae, fidelis animae et regnum coelestis gloriae.

Whom the angel said that He would have the seat of David; that is, the kingdom of holy Church, of the faithful soul and the kingdom of heavenly glory.

Cuius regni non erit finis, sicut Daniel praedixit, potestas eius potestas aeterna, quae non auferetur.

Whose kingdom will have no end as Daniel prophesied; Whose power will be everlasting power which will not be taken from Him.

Qui te fecit credere et prudenter modum facti inquirere, ut esses sacerdote Zacharia fidelior.

Who made thee to believe and prudently to inquire of the manner of the deed; that thou should be more faithful than Zechariah the priest.

Per quem Spiritus Sanctus supervenit in te, ut sua operatione conciperes et pareres te virgine permanente.

Through Whom the Holy Spirit overshadowed thee; that by His working thou should conceive and should give birth while remaining a Virgin.

Qui Christus, Dei virtus altissimi, id est Patris, obumbravit tibi, ut parias sine omni dolore.

Who is Christ, the power of the most high God, that is, the Father, overshadowed thee; that thou should give birth without any pain.

Qui tuus filius etiam Filius Dei est et ideo: Quod nascetur ex te sanctum, vocabitur Filius Dei.

Thy Son, Who is also Son of God and for this reason: that which will be born of thee will be holy and will be called Son of God.

SECUNDA
QUINQUAGENA

SECOND
PSALTER

Qui tibi sui praecursoris conceptum, proxime ex sterili nasciturum praenuntiavit.

Who made known to thee the conception of His precursor and that he would soon be born of a sterile womb.

Qui in cognatae conceptu, dum miraculum eius tuo iungitur, gaudium gaudio copulatur.

Who in the conception of thy relative, while her miracle was joined to thine, joy was coupled with joy.

A quo intus illustrata respondisti: "Ecce Domini mei ancilla, fiat mihi secundum verbum tuum".

By whom thou were inwardly enlightened to respond: "Behold the handmaid of my Lord. Let it be done unto me according to thy word."

Qui responsum tibi dedit, quod oraverunt patres, totus mundus

Who gave thee a response for which the fathers prayed and the deprecabatur; repondisti verbum, et Verbum ipsum concepisti.

whole world entreated. Thou did respond with a word and conceived the Word Himself.

55

Per cuius gratiam, omnem tuam oblita virtutem, de sola tua humilitate fateris te ancillam.

Through whose grace, forgetful of thy every virtue, out of thy humility alone thou professed thyself a handmaid.

56

Qui te Matrem Dei electam fecit mitem et humilem, quia mitem ipsum et humilem eras paritura.

Who made thee the chosen Mother of God, meek and humble for thou were to give birth to Him who is meek and humble.

57

Quem in eodem instanti, quo dixisti "Fiat mihi secundum verbum tuum", concepisti Deum in te hominem factum.

Whom thou did conceive, God made man in thee; and at the same instant thou did say, "Let it be done to me according to thy word."

Cum quo concepto exsurgens abisti in montana cum festinatione prae gaudio.

With Whom now conceived, thou rose up and went with haste to the hill country because of thy joy.

Qui paratam te fecit ministrare cognatae, sicut ipse de se dixit: "Non veni ministrari, sed ministrare."

Who made thee prepared to minister to thy relative, as He Himself said, "I did not come to be served but to serve."

Qui te dedit exemplum virginibus non circumcursare alienas domos, quae mansisti apud cognatam tribus mensibus.

Who gave thee as an example to virgins not to run around to strange homes; for thou did remain in the home of thy relative for three months.

Qui te salutante Elizabeth replevit Johannem Spiritu Sancto, ut in utero exsultaret.

Who, as Elizabeth greeted thee, filled John with the Holy Spirit, that he might rejoice in his mother's womb.

Qui duplici miraculo te et Elizabeth prophetare fecit, ut Elizabeth te benediceret.

Who in a twofold miracle made thee and Elizabeth to prophesy, so that Elizabeth might bless thee.

Qui tunc spiritum tuum fecit exsultare in Deo salutari et diffusius per Magnificat prophetare.

Who then made thy spirit exult in God thy Saviour and to utter prophecy far and wide through the Magnificat.

Qui fructus tui ventris prophetante Elizabeth est ab ea singulariter benedictus.

Who, the fruit of thy womb, was singularly blessed by Elizabeth in her prophecy.

Qui te matrem Domini a prophetissa Elizabeth statim voluit agnosci et nominari.

Who willed that thou should be known and declared Mother of the Lord by the prophetess Elizabeth.

Qui te a prophetissa Elizabeth, sicut eras, voluit beatam nominari, quia credidisti.

Who willed thee to be called blessed by the prophetess Elizabeth as indeed thou were, for thou did believe.

Qui te dignam fecit, ut uberius omnibus sanctis mulieribus per tuum Magnificat prophetasti.

Who made thee worthy and more so than all holy women, as thou prophesied through thy Magnificat.

Qui te propter mysterium et propter Johannis profectum fecit tribus mensibus manere.

Who on account of the mystery and of John's advancement made thee there to stay for three months.

Cum quo reversa esses in domum tuam, inventa es in utero habens de Spiritu Sancto.

With Whom thou had returned to thine own home and were found to be with child by the Holy Spirit.

De quo concepto Joseph adhuc ignarus mysterii te clam dimittere voluit.

Of Whose conception, Joseph, still ignorant of the mystery, wanted secretly to send thee away.

Qui te tristem non deseruit, sed Joseph per angelum instruxit Spiritus Sancti hoc opus esse.

Who did not desert thee in thy sadness; but through the angel instructed Joseph that this was the work of the Holy Spirit.

Quem per novem menses in tuo benedicto utero baiulasti et fovisti.

Whom for nine months thou carried and cherished in thy blessed womb.

Cum quo edicto Caesaris obediens ad profitendum in Bethlehem cum Joseph ivisti.

With Whom, obedient to the edict of Caesar, thou set out for Bethlehem with Joseph.

Cum quo illuc pervenisses, impleti sunt dies, ut illum pareres, et ibi eum peperisti.

With Whom when thou had arrived there, the days were fulfilled that thou might make Him known and there thou brought Him forth.

Quem pannis tuae paupertatis involvisti, ligans fasciis in praesepio locasti.

Whom thou wrapped with the garments of thy poverty; binding Him with swaddling clothes and laid Him in the manger.

Quem in medio duorum animalium super foenum paupercula reclinasti.

With Whom in poverty thou laid down on the hay between two animals.

Quem statim ut verum Deum adorasti dicens: "O salus et gaudium animae meae!"

Whom at once thou adored as true God saying, "O salvation and joy of my soul!"

Quem pastoribus angelus sub eadem hora nuntiavit natum, et totus angelicus exercitus voce consona canentes laudaverunt dicentes; "Gloria in excelsis Deo et in terra pax hominibus" etc.

Whose birth at the same hour the angel made known to the shepherds, and the whole angelic host praised in song with one voice saying, "Glory to God in the highest and on earth peace to men" etc.

Quem pastores festinantes invenerunt tecum et cum Joseph pannis involutum et positum in praesepio, et omnes, qui audierant, mirati sunt de his, quae pastores dixerunt.

Whom the shepherds in haste found, with thee and with Joseph, wrapped in swaddling clothes and placed in the manger, and all who had heard it marvelled at the things the shepherds had said.

De quo omnia verba, quae audieras, conservasti in corde tuo.	Whose every word spoken about Him thou treasured in thy heart.

Qui octava die circumcisus est, factus sub lege, ut nos omnes redimeret.	Who on the eighth day was circumcised according to the law, that He might redeem us all.

Qui eadam die vocatus est Jesus, quia erat verus salvator et verus Deus.	Who on the same day was called Jesus, for He is the true Saviour and true God.

Qui voluit, ut idem nomen prius ab angelo vocaretur, antequam in utero conciperetur, ut ostenderet se ante conceptum virgineum extitisse, ab aeterno in aeternum.	Who wanted that the same name be spoken by the angel before He was conceived in the Womb that He might show that He existed before the virginal conception; from eternity to eternity.

| Qui Jesus tertiadecima die a tribus regibus requisitus est et inventus et adoratus. | Who on the thirtieth day was sought by three kings and found and adored. |

| Cui regi, homini Deoque dona magi ferunt: aurum, thus er mirram. | To Whom as king, man and God the Magi offered as gifts: gold, incense and myrrh. |

| Qui die quadragesima cum oblatione pauperum ipse pauper in templo oblatus est. | Who on the fortieth day together with the offering of the poor, He, Himself poor, was offered in the Temple. |

| Quem Symeon suscepit in ulnas et benedixit, et sancta Anna superveniens confitebatur Dominus et loquebatur de eo omnibus, qui expectabant redemptionem Israel. | Whom Simeon took in his arms and blessed and Whom holy Anna, coming upon Him, confessed as Lord and spoke of Him to all who were waiting for the redemption of Israel. |

De quo Symeon prophetavit tibi: "Et tuam ipsius animam pertransibit gladius."

Concerning Whom Simeon prophesied to thee: "And a sword will pierce thy soul."

Cuius filii tui Passionem cum ipso semper dehinc in anima baiulasti.

Thy Son, Whose Passion from this point thou did always carry in thy soul.

Quem metu Herodis in Aegyptum deduxisti, illic habitans septem annis.

Whom, out of fear of Herod, thou led into Egypt; living there seven years.

Qui tunc implevit illud Isaiae: "Ascendet Dominus super nubem levem", id est: super te et intrabit Aegyptum.

Who then fulfilled that saying of Isaiah: "The Lord will go up on a light cloud," that is: upon thee and He will enter Egypt.

Quem post VII annos reduxisti in Nazareth, scilicet: florem in florem, tu flos mater floris.

Whom, after seven years, thou led back to Nazareth; namely, a flower to the flower, thou, a flower, mother of the flower.

Qui sicut tecum consuevit ad templum ascendere, tum anno XII° ibi remansit, ut daret exemplum posse filios Religionem intrare, et quia ipse doctor XII Apostolos voluerit ad praedicandum mittere.

Who, as He was accustomed to go up with thee to the Temple, then in His twelfth year remained there to give an example of how sons are able to enter Religion (religious life); and because He Himself as Teacher willed to send forth the Twelve Apostles to preach.

Quem quaesisti cum dolore, et reinvenisti in magno gaudio.

Whom thou did seek with sorrow, and found again with great joy.

Qui ex humilitate tibi fuit subditus, ut te excellentissima dignitate nobis praeponeret.

Who in humility was subject to thee; that He might place thee before us with the most excellent dignity.

Cuius verba et miracula conservasti, ut ea meditares et Evangelistis reservares.

Whose words and miracles thou kept; that thou might ponder them and preserve them for the Evangelists.

Qui anno tricesimo omnem implens humilitatem baptizatus fuit a servo.

Who in His thirtieth year, fulfilling all humility, was baptized by a servant.

Super quem vox Patris audita est: "Hic est Filius meus dilectus"; et Spiritus Sanctus est visus.

Above Whom the voice of the Father was heard: "This is My beloved Son"; and the Holy Spirit was seen.

| Quem Spiritus Sanctus duxit in desertum, ut tentaretur et vinceret diabolum. | Whom the Holy Spirit led into the desert; that He might be tempted and overcome the devil. |

| Qui tantus dux de te natus est, ut prodesset sua victoria ipse solus nobis omnibus. | Who was born of thee; so great a leader that His victory, won by Him alone, might benefit us all. |

TERTIA
QUINQUAGENA

THIRD
PSALTER

Qui ad tuas preces aquam in vinum mutavit.	Who at thy entreaties changed water into wine.

De quo dixisti ministris: "Quodcumque dixerit vobis, facite!" sciens ipsum piissimum.	Of Whom, knowing Him to be most dutiful, thou did say to the servants: "Do whatever He tells you."

Qui de Discipulis, quos elegit, duodecim Apostolos nominavit.	Who, from the Disciples that He chose, named twelve Apostles.

Qui eos octo beatitudines in monte sedens perdocuit.	Who, seated on the mount, thoroughly taught them the eight beatitudes.

Qui cum Discipulis Regnum coelorum praedicavit, circumeundo fatigatus ex itinere.	Who with the Disciples preached the Kingdom of God; going about tired from the journey.

Quem in sua patria sine honore habuerunt: Ipsum volentes de monte praecipitare.	Whom in His homeland they held without honour for they wanted to throw Him off a cliff.

Qui omnes infirmos sibi oblatos curavit, et tres mortuos suscitavit.	Who cured all the sick who were brought to Him, and raised three from the dead.

Quem Martha hospitio recepit, qui Mariam dilexit et Lazarum suscitavit et pro eo flevit.	Whom Martha received in her home and Who loved Mary and raised Lazarus for whom He wept.

Qui caecum a nativitate illuminavit, et in festo palmarum sedens in asello in Jerusalem venit.	Who enlightened the man who was blind from birth and on the feast of palms came into Jerusalem riding on a donkey.

Cui deinde acclamaverunt: "Miserere, fili David! Benedictus qui venit in nomine Domini!"

Whom then they acclaimed saying, "Son of David, have mercy! Blessed is He who comes in the name of the Lord!"

Qui mox templum intravit et ementes et vendentes inde eiecit.

Who then entered the Temple and expelled from it those who were buying and selling.

Cuius sanctissimos pedes Magdalena lacrimis lavit et capillis tersit.

Whose most holy feet Magdalene washed with her tears and dried with her hair.

Qui sacratissimum suum corpus et sanguinem in ultima Coena post lotionem pedum instituit consecrari et sumi in suam commemorationem in suae caritatis memoriale eximium.

Who at the Last Supper, after the washing of the feet, instituted His most holy Body and Blood to be consecrated and consumed in His memory in the exceptional memorial of His charity.

Qui post dulcissimum sermonem factum Discipulis ivit ad orationem cum ipsis.	Who, after He had given His sweetest discourse, went with His disciples to pray with them.

Qui segregatus a Discipulis, quantum est ictus lapidis, oravit et sanguinem sudavit.	Who, a stone's throw away from the Disciples, prayed and sweated blood.

Qui voluntatem suam in voluntatem Patris resignavit dicens: "Non mea, sed tua fiat!"	Who entrusted His will to the will of the Father saying, "Not My will, but Thine will be done!"

Qui ter Discipulos a somno excitavit et eos orare monuit, ne intrarent in tentationem.	Who roused up three Disciples from their sleep and admonished them to pray, that they enter not into temptation.

Qui hora Matutinali Judae et inimicis sponte obviam processit.	Who, at the hour of Matins, willingly went forth to meet Judas and His enemies.

Qui Judae dixit; "Amice, ad quid venisti?" et: "Juda, osculo filium hominis tradis?"	Who said to Judas, "Friend, why have thou come?" and "Judas, dost thou betray the Son of Man with a kiss?"

Qui dixisti inimicis: "Quem quaeritis?" et dicentibus "Jesum Nazarenum" respondisses: "Ego sum" abierunt retrorsum et ceciderunt in terram.	Who said to thine enemies: "Whom dost thou seek?" and to those who said, "Jesus of Nazareth" when Thou had answered, "I am He"; they drew back and fell to the ground.

Qui cum eos surgere permisses, te capi ab eis permisisti.

Who, when Thou did allow them to rise, allowed Thyself to be captured by them.

Qui, cum ligaverunt te, dixisti: "Tamquam ad latronem ad me venistis, cum cotidie apud vos essem in templo, et non me tenuistis; sed haec est hora vestra."

Who, when they bound Thee, did say, "You came to Me as to a thief, when daily I was with you in the temple and you did not take Me; but this is your hour."

Qui furibunde ligatus et per abrupta deductus ante Annam praesentabatur.

Who was furiously bound and through steep descents led away and presented before Annas.

Qui interrogatus dolose sed tu veridice respondisti, et pro hoc alapam suscepisti.

Who, though painfully interrogated, did answer truthfully and for this Thou did receive a slap.

Qui inde ad Caipham adductus, falsis testibus accusatus, facie velatus consputus, alapatus, derisus et morti reus adiudicatus fuit.

Who was then led to Caiaphas, accused by false witnesses, and Whose face was veiled with spittle, slapped, derided and judged guilty unto death.

Qui hora Prima ad Pilatum, de Pilato ad Herodem, et iterum de Herode, ubi interrogatus pie tacuit, ad Pilatum in veste alba remissus fuit.

Who at the First Hour was led to Pilate; from Pilate to Herod and again from Herod, where though interrogated He was reverently silent and was sent back to Pilate wearing a white garment.

Qui hora diei Tertia in domo Pilati flagellis caesus, spinis coronatus, purpura vestitus, consputus, in capite cum arundine percussus, omnia patienter sustinuit.

Who, at the Third hour of the day, in the house of Pilate was beaten with whips, crowned with thorns, dressed in purple, spat upon, beaten on the head with a reed; all of which He patiently bore.

Qui clamantibus judaeis "Crucifige, crucifige!" morti turpissimae adiudicatus est.

Who, as the Jews shouted "Crucify! Crucify!" was condemned to a most ignominious death.

Qui hora Sexta crucem per medium Jerusalem inter medios latrones portavit.

Who at the Sixth hour bore His cross, between two thieves, through the midst of Jerusalem.

Qui conversus ad te et ad mulieres, quae eum plangebant, eas de se consolabatur.

Who turned to thee and to the women who were lamenting Him, and consoled them concerning Himself.

Quem in monte vestibus dolorose exuerunt, et vino mirato potaverunt.

Whom on the mount they painfully stripped of His garments and to Whom they gave strange wine.

Qui manibus et pedibus cruci cum clavis grossis est affixus sine misericordia.

Whose hands and feet were mercilessly fixed to the cross with large nails.

Quem cum magna poena elevantes cum cruce, titulum superposuerunt.

Whom, with great pain they raised up with the cross and above they placed a sign.

Qui patientissime sustinens primo verbo pro crucifixoribus Patrem rogavit.

Who, bearing all with great patience, spoke His first word to the Father; praying for His crucifiers.

Qui latronem dextrum clementer exaudivit dicens: "Hodie mecum eris in Paradiso."

Who mercifully listened to the thief on the right saying, "Today, thou wilt be with Me in Paradise."

| Qui tibi moestissimae matri compatiens te Johanni commendavit. | Who, suffering in union with thee, His most sorrowful Mother, entrusted thee to John. |

| Qui hora Nona in cruce clamans: "Heloy, Heloy!" se quasi derelictum insinuavit. | Who, at the Ninth hour, on the cross crying "Eloi, Eloi!" manifested Himself as if forsaken. |

| Qui omnium salutem desiderans dixit "Sitio!" et cibatus est felle et aceto. | Who desiring the salvation of all, said, "I thirst!" and He was given gall and vinegar. |

| Qui, cum complesset omnia, quae de eo scripta erant, dixit: "Consummatum est." | Who, when He had fulfilled all that had been written about Him, said: "It is finished." |

Qui animam suam ponens, quando voluit, inclinato capite spiritum in manus Patris emisit.

Who, laying down His soul, when He willed it; having bowed His head, committed His spirit into the hands of the Father.

Cuius latus et cor lancea militis perforavit, et exiit sanguis et aqua.

Whose side and heart were pierced by the soldier's lance; and blood and water poured out.

Cuius corpus Joseph et Nicodemus deposuerunt et sepelierunt.

Whose body Joseph and Nicodemus took down and buried.

Cuius anima ad inferos descendit, et electos suos inde eripuit.

Whose soul descended to hell; and from there He took away His elect.

Qui die tertia resurrexit, et apparens te et suos laetificavit.	Who on the third day rose and appearing, He gave joy to thee and His disciples.

Qui quadragesima die ascendit, et die quinquagesima Spiritum Sanctum misit.	Who ascended on the fortieth day, and on the fiftieth day sent the Holy Spirit.

Qui te de post inter Apostolos et Evangelistas et Discipulos conversari fecit.	Who afterwards made thee to live among the Apostles and Evangelists and Disciples.

Qui te a Johanne specialius usque ad finem vitae venerari et custodiri fecit.	Who made thee to be venerated and watched over in a more special manner by John till the end of thy life.

Quem prae nimio amore saepius in spiritu visitasti ita ibi habitans, ut adire posses Ascensionis eius vestigia, et locum sepulturae ac Resurrectionis, seu omnia, in quibus est passus filius tuus, loca invisere.

Whom, because of thy great love in spirit thou visited more often; thus living there that thou might go to the footsteps of His Ascension and the place of His burial and Resurrection, or to visit all the places where thy Son did suffer.

Qui te festivus in morte cum omnibus Sanctis visitavit, et primo animam, tandem tertia die simul cum corpore te ad se assumens elevavit super omnes choros Angelorum, ut speciem vultumque posses videre Salvatoris.

Who in joy visited thee in death with all the Saints; and first thy soul and then on the third day together with thy body, assumed thee to Himself above all the choirs of Angels, that thou might see the beauty and face of the Saviour.

Qui venturus est iudicare vivos et mortuos, qui iudicatus est iniuste a Judaeis in anima mortuis.

Who will come to judge the living and the dead; He Who was unjustly judged by the Jews who are not living in spirit.

Concluding Oration

Hunc igitur, o sancta Dei genetrix, ora pro omnibus, et pro nobis, qui hoc psalterium tibi pie deprompsimus, sperantes per te a filio tuo mercedem spiritualem et praesentem prosperitatem simul et vitam aeternam, quae honorasti semper honorantes te et optime nosti in tempore opportuno resalutare te modo salutantes in diebus salutis et gratiae.

Therefore, O holy Mother of God, pray for all and for us who have piously offered thee this Psalter; hoping through thee to obtain from thy Son spiritual benefit and prosperity now, as well as eternal life. For thou always do honour those who honour thee; and have known in the proper time to return the greeting of those who greet thee now in the days of salvation and grace.

Sed etiam nunc te saluto hac aurea tua salutatione, quam didici a devoto Carthusiensi:

And now I greet thee with this golden greeting which I learned from a devout Carthusian:

Ave, Maria, gratia plena,	*Hail Mary, full of grace,*
quia Verbum in te caro factum est	for the Word became flesh in thee,
Dominus tecum	*The Lord is with thee*
et habitabit in nobis,	and He dwelt among us.
Benedicta tu in mulieribus,	*Blessed art thou among women,*
ex te vidimus gloriam eius;	from thee we saw His glory:
Et benedictus fructus ventris tui,	*And blessed is the fruit of thy womb,*
gloriam quasi Unigeniti a Patre:	the glory as it were of the Only Begotten Son of the Father:
Jesum Christum	*Jesus Christ*
plenum gratiae et veritatis.	full of grace and truth.
Amen.	*Amen.*